Square Eyes

written by Karen Tayleur
illustrated by Gus Gordon

Desk Copy Request / Information

To place your desk copy request or for more information,
please contact the following office:
Tel : (02) 3273-4300   Fax : (02) 3273-4303

Contents

Welcome to Magic Reader

Character sketches provide prior information about the main characters

Repetitive and straightforward story lines

Predictable format

Familiar content related to everyday experiences

Full-color illustrations

Simply constructed sentences

A variety of simple sentence patterns

Includes oral and written language patterns

Use of high-frequency words

How to Use Magic Reader

Step 1. Listen to the Story

You'll love listening to the audio as you follow the flow of the story, even if you don't understand every single word or sentence.

Step 2. Read along with the Story

While improving your pronunciation and your ability to memorize sentences, you'll build confidence as you listen to and then read along with the audio in a loud voice.

Step 3. Listen to Specific Parts of Each Chapter

With each chapter broken up into sections, you'll be able to fully understand the meaning of each part as you listen.

Step 4. Try the Activity Questions

Make sure you fully understand the meaning of each story by doing the accompanying exercises.

Characters 

Marcus can't stop watching TV. His favorite show is about cooking.

Tula likes skateboards, computers, and having fun.

Chapter One

Watching TV

Marcus Todd had square eyes. Well, he didn't really have square eyes. But he did spend all his time watching TV. Except, of course, when he was at school. Or in the shower. Or asleep.

His parents said, "Marcus Todd, you will get square eyes if you don't stop watching TV." But Marcus didn't care.

He didn't want to help his mother with
her pottery.

He never felt like making model cars
with his father.

The boy next door asked Marcus to come outside to play. "No thanks," said Marcus. "Maybe later."

That was what he always said. But there never was a later. The boy next door got tired of asking him.

Chapter Two

Bang! Sizzle! Broken!

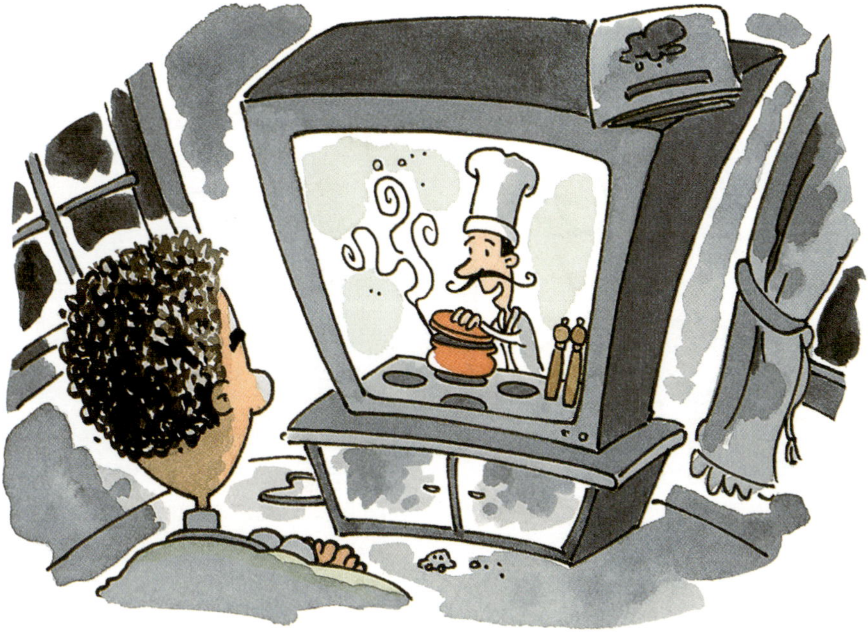

One night, Marcus climbed out of bed and turned on the TV. He kept the sound down. He sat close to the TV screen. He watched his favorite show.

The TV show was all about cooking.
Creamy soups. Perfect pasta. Amazing
cakes.

Marcus thought the food on TV looked
delicious. He wished his parents could cook
food like that. They both cooked lots of
chicken and boring vegetables.

The next morning, Marcus had trouble getting out of bed. He had stayed up too late watching TV. His brain was too bleary for school. He even fell asleep at his desk.

"Have you finished your worksheet, Marcus?" his teacher asked.

"Half a cup of plain flour," Marcus mumbled. The class laughed.

That afternoon, something terrible happened. Marcus Todd's TV broke. It went BANG! Then SIZZLE! Then nothing.

"MOM!" Marcus yelled. His mother rushed into the room. Marcus pointed to the blank TV screen.

"Oh dear," said his mother. "That's the end of that." She went back to her pottery.

"DAD!" yelled Marcus.

His father saw the TV and shook his head. "Broken," he said. "Overworked."

"Can you please fix it?" Marcus begged.

But his father had already left the room.

"Great," said Marcus. "Now what am I going to do?"

Marcus sat and watched the TV out of habit. He stared at the blank screen until he got bored.

"I'm going to the park," he called to his mom as he went out the door.

Chapter Three

A New Friend

There were plenty of kids at the park. They were all playing games and having fun. Marcus decided to join in. He saw some kids from school flying a kite. He didn't know how to fly a kite.

Some kids were playing tag. Marcus

had never played tag in his whole life.

He wasn't very good at games.

Everything he knew about was on TV.

Marcus Todd sat by himself in the park.

He sat at one end of a seesaw and thought

about the TV show he was missing.

Then WHOOSH! Marcus nearly flew
off the seesaw. Up went his seat high
into the air. Marcus looked down at the
other end of the seesaw. A girl with dark
hair was sitting there.

"Hi," said the girl.

"Hello," said Marcus.

"You can't do this by yourself," said the
girl. She pointed to the seesaw.

"You're right," Marcus said.

Marcus wanted to get off the seesaw.
But his feet were high off the ground.

"Isn't it your turn?" said Marcus.

"My turn?" asked the girl.

Marcus pointed at the ground. The girl laughed and pushed herself up. Slowly, Marcus came down to the ground.

"Thanks," he said. "My name's Marcus Todd. What's your name?"

"Tula. Tula Marika Veradis," she said.
"Mrs. Maxwell's class, Room 8,
Marysville Elementary."

Then she jumped off the seesaw. She
picked up her skateboard and started to
walk away.

"Mrs. Maxwell's class, Room 8?" yelled Marcus. "That's my class."

"Right," Tula agreed.

Marcus didn't know what to say.

"Got to go," said Tula. "Class project,
remember?" She kept walking.

"Class project?" Marcus yelled after her.
"What class project?"

Marcus ran after Tula. It was hard work because she walked fast. "Tula, wait," he puffed, out of breath.

Tula let him catch up.

Chapter Four

The Perfect Project

"My project's really cool," said Tula. "I've been working on it for ages. Haven't you started? It's due tomorrow."

She put her skateboard on the ground and gave it a kick with her foot. The skateboard flipped into her hand.

"Maybe you were asleep in class. You do that a lot," said Tula. She flipped her skateboard again. "Are you sick or something? "

"No," said Marcus, looking at the skateboard. "I just need lots of sleep."

"My mom knows your mom," said
Tula. "And your mom said that you
watch TV. A lot."

"So?" Marcus felt his face get hot.

"So, your mom told my mom. That's
all." Tula flipped her skateboard. "TV's
okay." She threw him the skateboard.
"Do you want a try?" she asked.

Marcus held the skateboard in his hands. He put it on the ground. He kicked at it with his foot like Tula. It flew up and hit him on the leg.

"Ow!" he said. "I've never done this before. It's tricky."

"Hey, that's pretty good for your first time," said Tula.

"Anyway," said Tula. "Class project.
Due tomorrow. I chose surfing."

Marcus kicked at the skateboard again.
He nearly caught it this time.

"What are you going to do?" said Tula.

"I don't even know where to start,"
said Marcus.

"Do you have any hobbies?" asked
Tula.

Marcus tried to think of a hobby-a
hobby besides watching TV.

Then Marcus had an idea. "I could do it on cooking," he said.

"What can you cook?" asked Tula.

"Everything," said Marcus. He kicked at the skateboard. It fell over.

"Wow," said Tula. "That's great. I can't cook at all."

Marcus went home. "I've got a project to do," he told his mother. "Could I please use the kitchen?"

His mother looked surprised. "Of course," she said. "But what are you going to do?"

"You'll see," said Marcus.

Chapter Five

MR-G3-28
MP3

A Piece of Cake

Marcus decided to make a cake. He'd seen someone make a cake on TV. It looked easy. He got out all the ingredients and mixed them in a bowl. Then he poured the mixture into a cake pan.

Later, Marcus and his mother pulled a very flat, mushy mess out of the oven.

Marcus phoned Tula. "Something awful has happened," he said.

"What is it?" asked Tula.

"I've just discovered I can't cook!" cried Marcus. "Can you help?"

"I'll be right over," said Tula.

Marcus was waiting at the kitchen table when Tula arrived.

"Where's your cookbook?" she asked.

"You need a book?" asked Marcus. "Can't you just tell me what to do?"

Tula laughed "I can't cook, remember," she said. "You need a recipe. From a cookbook."

Marcus searched until he found a
cookbook. It was propping up one leg of
the kitchen table. He started again and
followed the recipe. Step by step. Finally,
he popped a new cake into the oven.

The next morning, the teacher asked Marcus to talk about his project. Marcus opened the lid of a large cardboard box and lifted out a huge chocolate cake.

It wasn't a perfect cake. A broken piece was stuck on with icing. But the whole class thought it was very tasty. And Marcus was very proud.

That night, Marcus Todd went to bed

without even once thinking about TV.

EXERCISES

Name ___________________

Who did what?

Complete each sentence by using your copy of Square Eyes to find out who did what.

_______________________________ got tired of asking him.

_______________________________ thought the food on TV looked delicious.

The next morning, _________________ had trouble getting out of bed.

_______________________________ rushed into the room.

But _________________ had already left the room.

_________________ had never played tag in his whole life.

_________________ was sitting there.

_________________ let him catch up.

_________________ flipped her skateboard.

_______________________ held the skateboard in his hands.

Then _________________ had an idea.

Later, ___________________ pulled a very flat, mushy mess out of the oven.

___________________ was waiting at the kitchen table when ___________________ arrived.

The next morning, ___________________ asked Marcus to talk about his project.

Other words for "said"

Sometimes the word "said" is used too many times in writing. In Square Eyes there are some different words used instead of the word "said." These words, such as "yelled," "begged" and "called," all add information about the way the person is feeling. Here are some examples:

"MOM!" Marcus yelled.

"Can you please fix it?" Marcus begged.

"I'm going to the park," he called to his mom as he went out the door.

*Below is a list of words that you can us in your own writing.
Use these words to write another Marcus Todd adventure.*

asked	chatted
added	warned
grumbled	agreed
murmured	whispered
yelled	cried
argued	explained
joked	answered
wept	smiled

Character profile

Choose a character from Square Eyes and answer the following questions about them.

Character's name _______________________________.

What does this character look like? (Use the illustrations to help you.)

____

____

____

____

What does this character do?

____

____

____

____

____

____

What does the author tell us about this character?

____

____

____

____

What are some of the things this character says?

____

____

____

____

Draw a portrait of your chosen character and display it with this sheet.

Glossary

pottery `n.` the act of making bowls, dishes, cups, vases, etc. with clay

He didn't want to help his mother with pottery.

creamy `adj.` soft and smooth, having cream

Creamy soups. Perfect pasta.

bleary `adj.` blurry due to sleepiness or weariness

His brain was too bleary for school.

rush (-rushed) `v.` to move or act quickly

His mother rushed into the room.

blank `adj.` empty, having nothing

Marcus pointed at the blank TV screen.

overwork (-overworked) `v.` to use too much

"Broken," he said. "Overworked."

beg (-begged) `v.` to ask someone to give or do something

"Can you fix it?" Marcus begged.

join (-joined) `v.` to do something with others

Marcus decided to join in.

Glossary

tag [n.] a children's game where one person chases the others and tries to touch them.

Some kids were playing tag.

skateboard [n.] a small vehicle with four wheels that you ride by standing on it

She picked up her skateboard and started to walk away.

puff (-puffed) [v.] to breath quickly and heavily after using energy

"Tula, wait," he puffed, out of breath.

flip (-flipped) [v.] to turn over

The skateboard flipped into her hand.

ingredient [n.] one of the things required to make something

He got out all the ingredients and mixed them in a bowl.

recipe [n.] instructions that show you how to make something, usually food

"You need a recipe."

prop (-propped) [v.] to hold up

It was propping up one leg of the kitchen table.

Author: Karen Tayleur

Karen Tayleur thinks cooking is the greatest thing to do in the world—when you're in the mood. Otherwise she'd rather be doing anything else but. Her favorite pastime is to lie on the couch with a bowl of fresh popcorn watching television—preferably a cooking show where someone else does the cooking. Of course, after all that popcorn, her second favorite pastime is reading diet books...

Illustrator: Gus Gordon

Gus is a full-time silly picture drawer. He has drawn silly pictures just about anywhere that silly pictures go, including eighteen silly kids' books. His favorite characters to draw are chickens, loonies and spooky people but he's not sure why!